C0-EDX-857

About the Author™

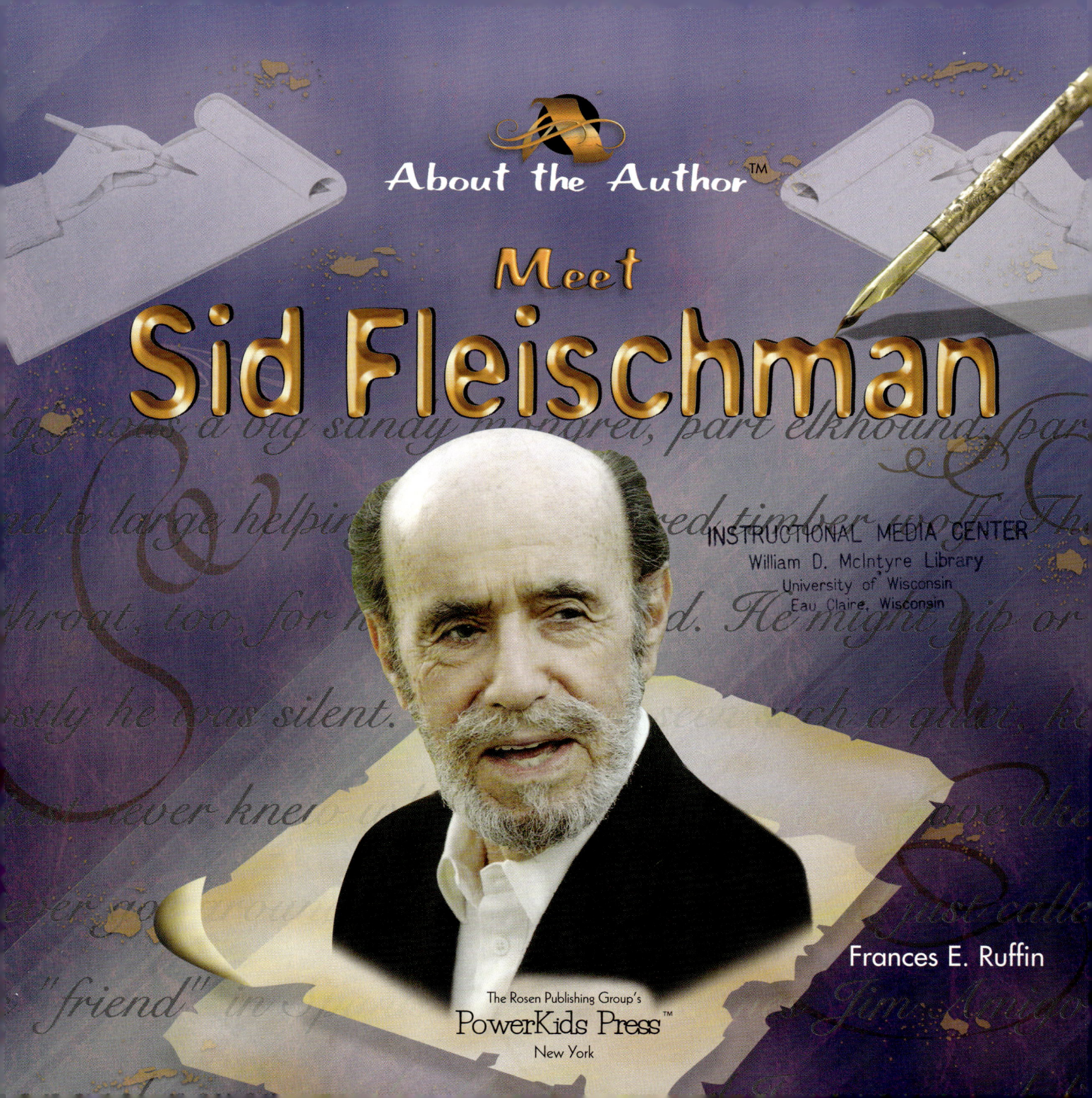

Meet
Sid Fleischman

Frances E. Ruffin

The Rosen Publishing Group's
PowerKids Press™
New York

For Timothy, who has experienced the magic of being on stage

Published in 2006 by The Rosen Publishing Group, Inc.
29 East 21st Street, New York, NY 10010

Copyright © 2006 by The Rosen Publishing Group, Inc.

All rights reserved. No part of this book may be reproduced in any form without permission in writing from the publisher, except by a reviewer.

First Edition

Editor: Rachel O'Connor
Book Design: Julio A. Gil
Photo Researcher: Cindy Reiman

Photo Credits: All photos provided by Sid Fleischman. Cover photo by Kevin O'Malley.

Grateful acknowledgment is made for permission to reprint previously published material:
p. 5 From THE 13TH FLOOR: A GHOST STORY by Sid Fleischman. Text copyright © 1995 by Seymour Fleischman. Used by permission of HarperCollins Publishers.
pp. 11, 12 (pamphlet), 16 (bottom) From THE ABRACADABRA KID by Sid Fleischman. Copyright © 1996 by Sid Fleischman. Used with the permission of Greenwillow Books. Used by permission of HarperCollins Publishers.
p. 14 From JIM UGLY by Sid Fleischman. Used by permission of HarperCollins Publishers.
p. 21 From THE WHIPPING BOY by Sid Fleischman. Copyright © 1988 by Sid Fleischman. Illustrations Copyright © 1988 by Peter Sis. Used by permission of HarperCollins Publishers.

Library of Congress Cataloging-in-Publication Data

Ruffin, Frances E.
  Meet Sid Fleischman / Frances E. Ruffin.
      p. cm. — (About the author)
  Includes index.
  ISBN 1-4042-3132-3 (lib. bdg.)
 1. Fleischman, Sid, 1920– —Juvenile literature. 2. Authors, American—20th century—Biography—Juvenile literature. 3. Children's stories—Authorship—Juvenile literature. I. Title. II. Series.

  PS3556.L42269Z86 2006
  813'.54—dc22

2005001735

Manufactured in the United States of America

Contents

1	A Writer's Life	5
2	A Move West	6
3	Two Passions	9
4	The Magician	10
5	Show Business	13
6	Learning to Write	14
7	In the Navy	17
8	Writing for Children	18
9	The Newbery Medal	21
10	In His Own Words	22
	Glossary	23
	Index	24
	Web Sites	24

Sid Fleischman served in the U.S. Navy during World War II. He served from 1941 until the end of the war in 1945. You can see Sid here showing his fellow sailors some card tricks. The war is over and they are all happy to be going home.

A Writer's Life

Writer Sid Fleischman's life has provided him with great **material** for the wonderfully witty and wise books that he writes for children. His **experiences** included traveling as a magician in his teen years. He searched for gold in the mountains of California, and he served in the U.S. Navy during **World War II**. For a time he was a newspaper reporter.

Sid wrote his first book, which was about magic tricks, while he was in high school. Today he is an award-winning author of 59 books for children and adults. Young readers enjoy Sid's funny tall tales in the McBroom series, his ghost stories, such as *The 13th Floor*, and a long list of books that take the reader on great adventures.

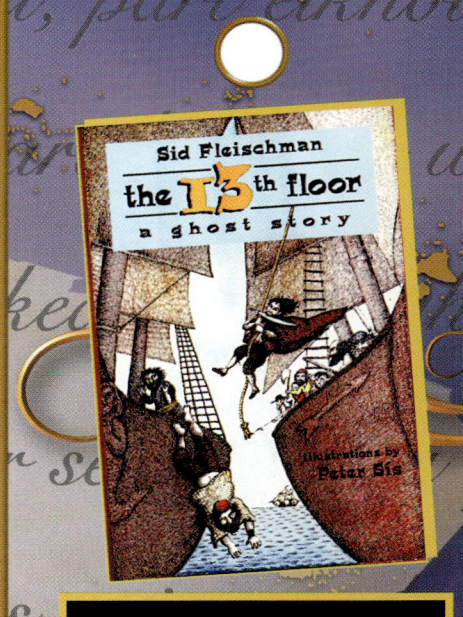

"When I reached the twelfth floor, I slowed the elevator to a crawl. I continued upward, inch by inch. . . . But before long, I saw the number 14 appear in the peep window. The thirteenth floor wasn't there."

—From p. 19, The 13th Floor

A Move West

Sid was born in Brooklyn, New York, on March 16, 1920. His father, Reuben, was from the Ukraine. His mother, Sadie, was born in New York, but her parents came from Lithuania and England. When he was born, Sid was named Avrom Zalmon. Later his mother changed it to Albert Sidney. Everyone called him Sid. He had an older sister, Pearl, and a younger sister, Honey.

When Sid was a baby, the Fleischmans moved across the country. Sid's father, who was a tailor, thought that he might make a better living on the West Coast. Sid's father moved the family to San Diego, California.

Sid and his father are shown together on a beach in San Diego. San Diego was the repair base for the U.S. Navy's Eleventh Fleet. Sid's father opened a shop there that sold uniforms and other items that the sailors might need.

Two-year-old Sid (right) enjoys the California sun with his mother and sister Pearl.

Sid performs a magic trick at the age of 15. He is doing his best to look mysterious.

Two Passions

As a young boy, Sid had two great **passions**. The first was for the story of Robin Hood, a bandit who was known to steal from the rich to give to the poor. Sid often made bows and arrows from sticks that he found. He pretended that he lived the life of his hero in Sherwood Forest.

His second passion was for magic, and this passion continues today. A visit to a **sideshow** when he was in the fifth grade changed his life. One of the acts in the show featured a man doing magic tricks with a ball. The man also did tricks with a deck of cards. Sid was excited by the magic acts he had seen. More than anything, Sid knew that he wanted to be a magician.

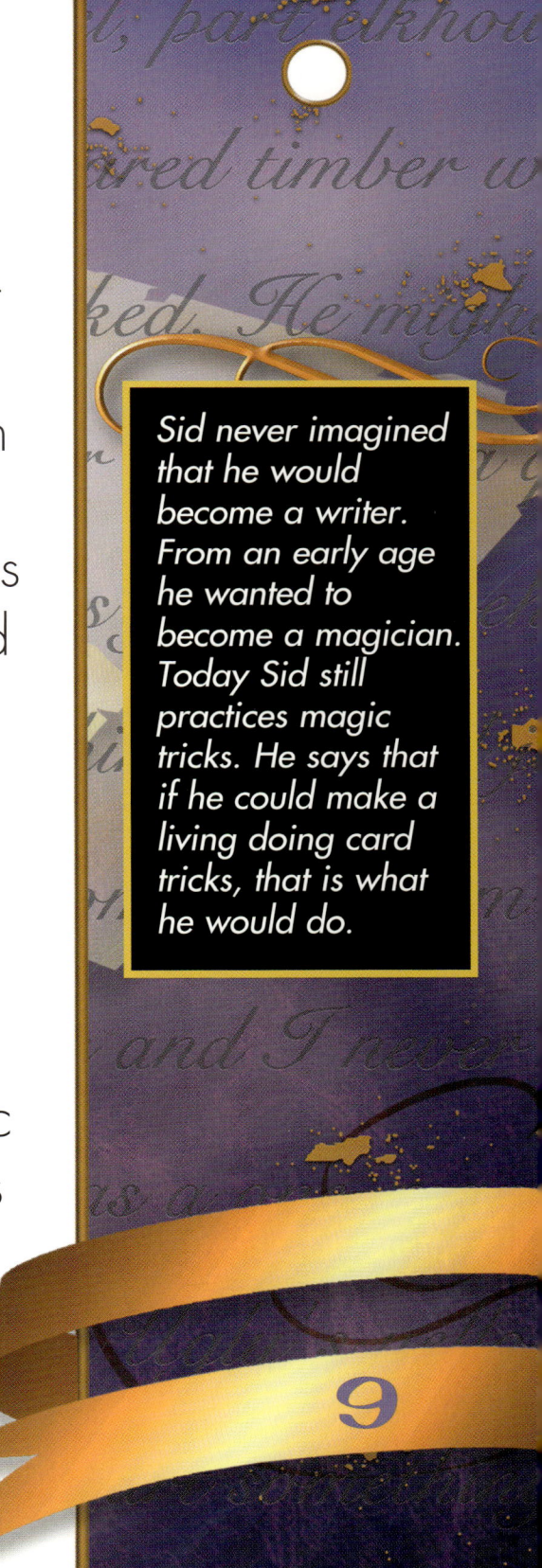

Sid never imagined that he would become a writer. From an early age he wanted to become a magician. Today Sid still practices magic tricks. He says that if he could make a living doing card tricks, that is what he would do.

The Magician

Sid taught himself how to **perform** magic tricks. He read any book about magic and magicians that he could get his hands on from the San Diego public library. Sid had a shoe box in which he stored **props** for his magic tricks.

One day he saw an ad in a newspaper about a meeting of the San Diego Magicians Club. He went to the place where the magicians met. The president of the club, Professor Charles Fait, told him that they did not give memberships to boys. Sid was 14 years old and shy, but he was **determined** to become a member.

He showed the man some of his tricks and proved to the president that he was a serious magician.

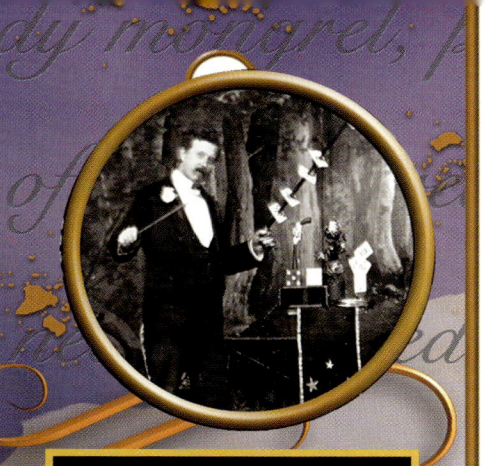

Professor Fait, shown here, loved to tell tall tales and do magic tricks at the same time. His stories inspired Sid to write tall tales. Sid wrote a number of books about a character named Josh McBroom. McBroom was a farmer who had a wife and 11 children. They all lived on a 1-acre (.4 ha) farm with soil so rich that it grew three crops of pumpkins a day!

Once Sid became a member of the San Diego Magicians Club, a boy named Buddy Ryan was allowed to join. Sid (right) and Buddy (left) formed a friendship that lasted almost 40 years.

Sid and Buddy called their traveling show See'n Is Believ'n. They traveled throughout California in a car they had bought for $38. They performed in army camps, lodges, and movie theaters. Inset: Sid printed flyers advertising their show in his high school print shop class.

Show Business

During the summer of 1936, Sid Fleischman and Buddy Ryan became traveling magicians. They had a lot of tricks and two suitcases filled with props, including magic coins, silk scarves, and wands. Sid changed his name for their act when they decided to call themselves The Ryan Brothers. He thought it sounded better than using two names. The show was called See'n Is Believ'n.

Sid **graduated** from high school in 1938, and he continued to follow his dream. He found a job in **vaudeville** at the Hippodrome Theater in Los Angeles. He performed three days a week, five shows a day. He was paid $15 a week.

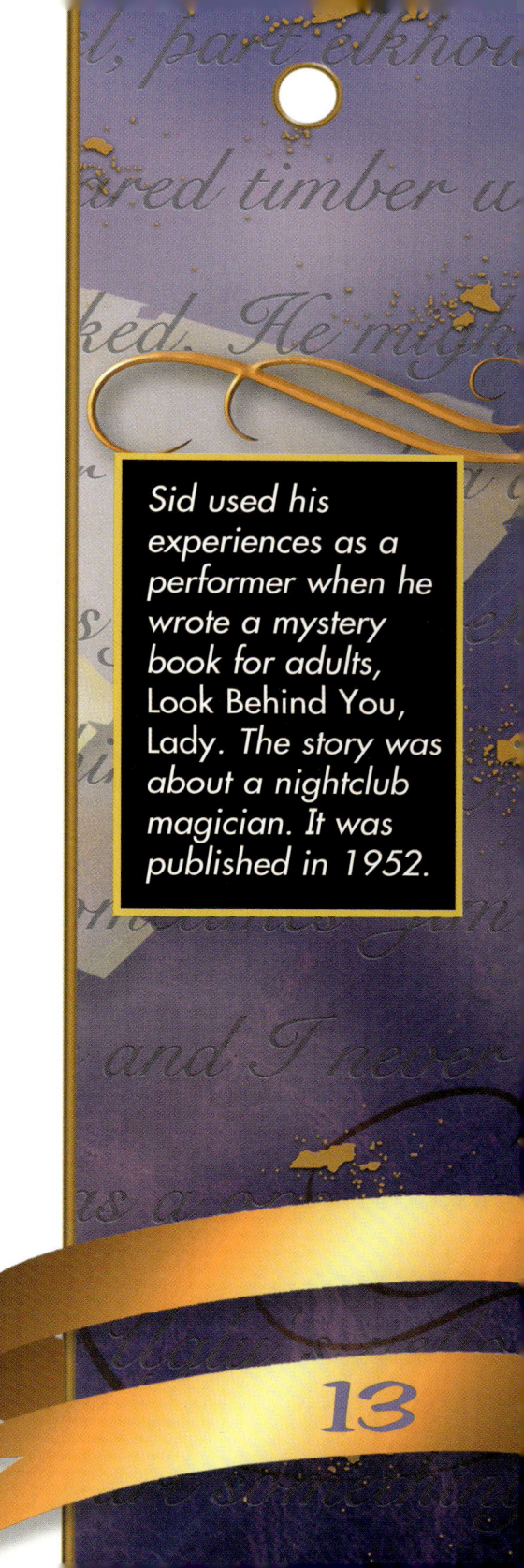

Sid used his experiences as a performer when he wrote a mystery book for adults, Look Behind You, Lady. *The story was about a nightclub magician. It was published in 1952.*

Learning to Write

When Sid was not performing, he enjoyed reading short stories, especially those that had surprise endings. Sid was also interested in writing. While he was a senior in high school, he wrote a book called *Between Cocktails*. It was a book that described how to do magic tricks. When he was 19, he sent the book to a **publisher** and it was published. Sid said that seeing his book in print changed everything. He began to think about becoming a writer.

Sid left the show that he had been traveling with and entered San Diego State College. He enrolled in a **literature** class, which taught him a new way of reading. This helped Sid become a better writer.

> "It seemed to me my dad should have made sure I knew he was alive and fit. He shouldn't have let Axie keep the secret to himself. He shouldn't have played a trick like that on me."
>
> —From p. 43, *Jim Ugly*

In his literature class at San Diego State College, Sid discovered new wonders in reading. Inset: Here you can see pages from Sid's book *Between Cocktails.* Sid used his own hands for the photos.

Top: *Sid and Betty got married when he was 21 and she was 20. Here they are shortly after they married.* Bottom: *Sid served on this U.S. Navy ship, the DE 447. During the war Sid served in the Far East and the South Pacific.*

In the Navy

While Sid was studying at San Diego State, America entered World War II. Sid joined the U.S. Navy Reserves and was called for duty in 1941. Before leaving he married Betty Taylor, a student he had been dating in college. Sid then shipped out on the USS *Albert T. Harris*. He was in the navy until the war ended in 1945. After the war Sid began to write mystery and **suspense novels**. He returned to college and graduated in 1949. He worked briefly as a reporter for the *San Diego Daily Journal* newspaper until the paper closed in 1950. By this time he had published his first novel. By 1963, Sid had published 10 novels, including *Yellowleg* and *Blood Alley*.

Sid believes that writers have a responsibility to do their best work for their young readers. He has said, "The books we enjoy as children stay with us forever."

Writing for Children

Sid and Betty had three children. They were Jane, Paul, and Anne. Sid was working full-time as a writer. When he realized that his young children did not understand what he did for a living, he began to write a book just for them. The book was called *Mr. Mysterious & Company*. Published in 1962, the book was about a magician and his family. Sid based the characters on his children, though he gave them different names. Sid said the book helped him find a **comic** writer's voice. After he finished each chapter, Sid would read it to Betty and the kids, hoping to make them laugh. Sid continued to write children's books that were funny, such as *Bandit's Moon* and *Disappearing Act*.

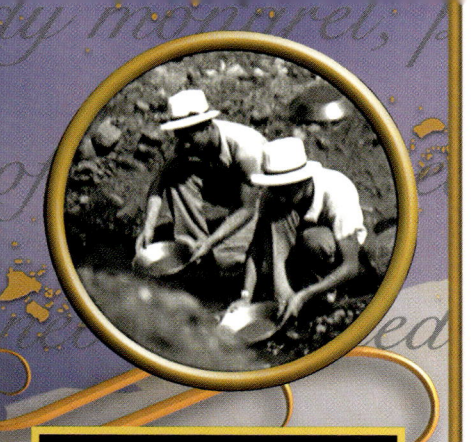

When Sid (right) and his friend Buddy (left) were teenagers they performed in California's tiny gold-mining towns. While they were there, they also took time to pan for gold hoping to get rich. His experiences panning for gold became part of his novel By the Great Horn Spoon! *It is a story about the California gold rush.*

Anne (seated), Jane, and Paul gave their father suggestions when he was writing *Mr. Mysterious & Company,* the book that was based on them.

Sid is shown here wearing the Newbery Medal around his neck. The Newbery Medal is given once a year by the American Library Association. It is the most important award, or honor, given for children's literature.

The Newbery Medal

One morning in January 1987, Sid learned that he had won the Newbery Medal for his children's novel *The Whipping Boy*. This is a story about a poor boy who is sent to live in the palace of a royal family. Whenever the very bratty prince misbehaved, the poor boy was spanked instead of the prince. A royal child could not be punished, or corrected. The story is funny, but it is also a serious story about friendship and being accountable for one's actions. Sid spent 10 years writing the book. Luckily for his readers, his other books took a lot less time to write. When asked which of his books is his favorite, Sid says he usually loves the book he has just finished!

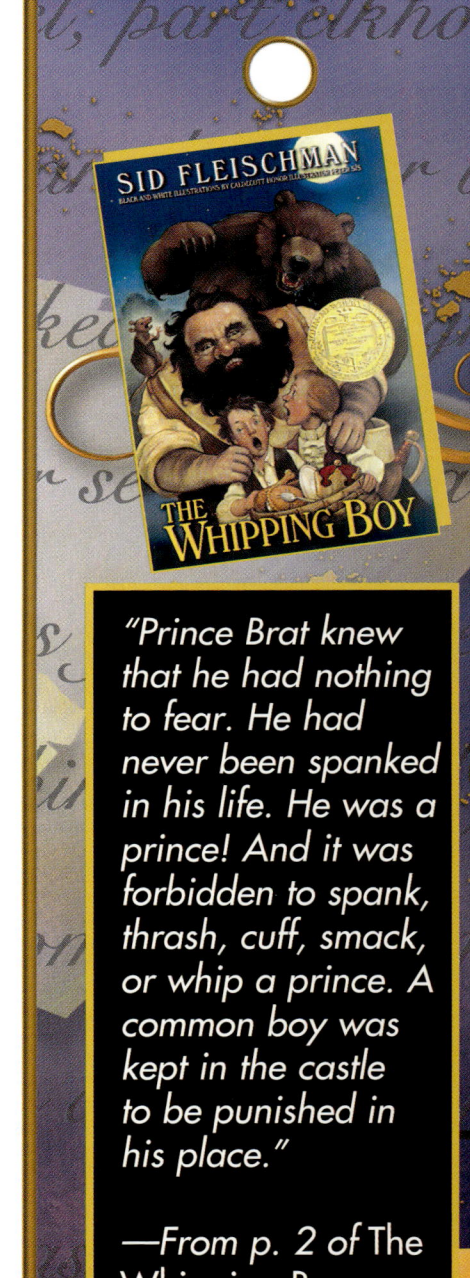

> "Prince Brat knew that he had nothing to fear. He had never been spanked in his life. He was a prince! And it was forbidden to spank, thrash, cuff, smack, or whip a prince. A common boy was kept in the castle to be punished in his place."
>
> —From p. 2 of *The Whipping Boy*

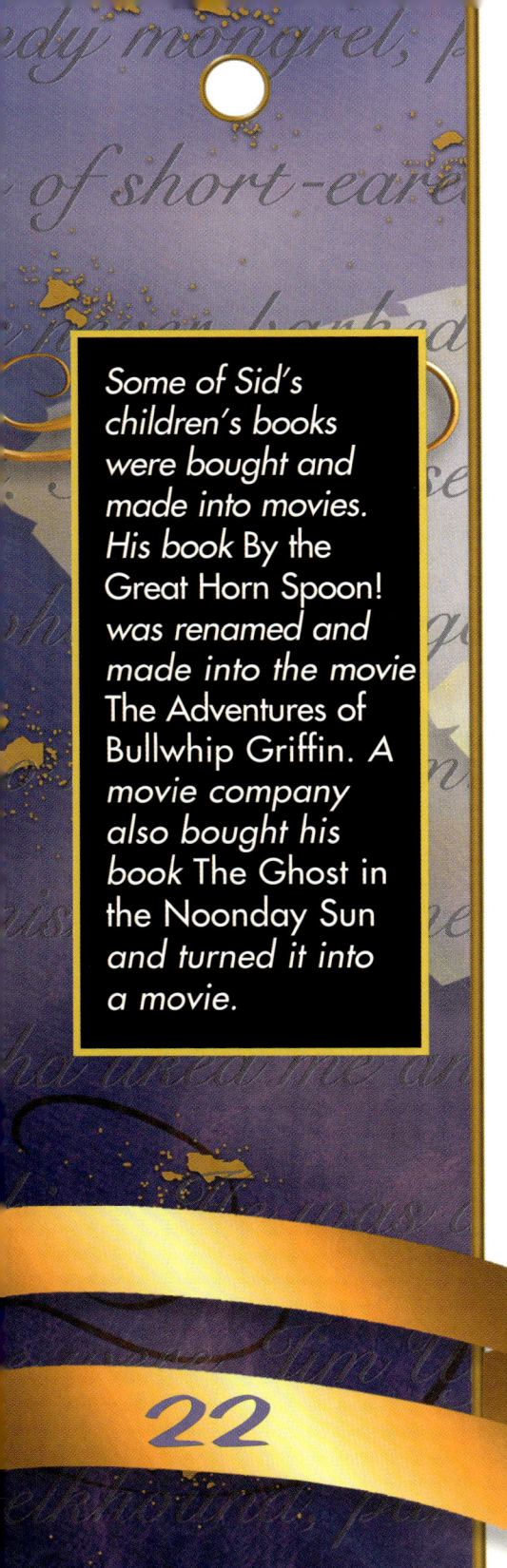

In His Own Words

Some of Sid's children's books were bought and made into movies. His book By the Great Horn Spoon! *was renamed and made into the movie* The Adventures of Bullwhip Griffin. *A movie company also bought his book* The Ghost in the Noonday Sun *and turned it into a movie.*

What did it feel like to win the Newbery?
It was as stunning as being struck by lightning. I didn't know my novel *The Whipping Boy* was being considered.

How long did it take you to write *The Whipping Boy*?
More than 10 years. I got off on the wrong track and was very slow to discover my mistake. Once I came to my senses, the story wrote rather quickly. Six or seven months, as I recall.

How many other books have you written?
I don't know. Fifty or 60, something like that. But not all were written for children. When I was a young writer and didn't know any better, I wrote novels for adults.

Does it always take you ages to write a book?
Some writers are fast. Some are slow. Most of us are both. Sometimes everything works and the writing gallops along. My tall tales about the McBroom family, each 15 or so typed pages, take me up to three months. That's galloping for me. When I start a novel, I know that I'm going to be at the computer for the next year or two or three.

Where do you get your ideas?
I wish I knew. They seem to be everywhere and nowhere. The problem is figuring out what to do with the idea once it takes possession of you.

Glossary

comic (KAH-mik) Funny.
determined (dih-TER-mind) Being very fixed on doing something.
experiences (ik-SPEER-ee-ents-iz) Things that a person has done or seen.
graduated (GRAH-joo-wayt-ed) To have finished a course of school.
literature (LIH-tuh-ruh-chur) Writings such as books, plays, and poetry.
material (muh-TEER-ee-ul) What something is made of.
medal (MEH-dul) A small, round piece of metal that is given as a prize.
novels (NAH-vulz) Long stories about made-up people and events.
passions (PA-shunz) Very strong feelings.
perform (per-FORM) To sing, dance, act, or play an instrument in front of other people.
props (PROPS) Things that are used to hold something in place.
publisher (PUH-blih-shur) A person or company whose business is printing and selling books, newspapers, or magazines.
sideshow (SYD-shoh) A small show that is part of a larger show.
suspense (suh-SPENS) Having to do with not knowing the outcome of an event.
vaudeville (VAHD-vel) Stage shows that presented many acts, including comedians, magicians, singers, and other entertainers.
World War II (WURLD WOR TOO) A war fought by the United States, Great Britain, France, and the Soviet Union against Germany, Japan, and Italy from 1939 to 1945.

Index

B
Between Cocktails, 14

F
Fait, Charles, 10
Fleischman, Anne (daughter), 18
Fleischman, Betty Taylor (wife), 17, 18
Fleischman, Honey (sister), 6
Fleischman, Jane (daughter), 18
Fleischman, Paul (son), 18
Fleischman, Pearl (sister), 6
Fleischman, Reuben (father), 6
Fleischman, Sadie (mother), 6

M
McBroom series, 5
Mr. Mysterious & Company, 18

N
Newbery Medal, 21

R
Ryan, Buddy, 13

S
San Diego Magicians Club, 10
San Diego State College, 14, 17

T
13th Floor, The, 5

W
Whipping Boy, The, 21
World War II, 5, 17

Web Sites

Due to the changing nature of Internet links, PowerKids Press has developed an online list of Web sites related to the subject of this book. This site is updated regularly. Please use this link to access the list: www.powerkidslinks.com/aa/sidfleis/